"No will – no say"

A simple guide to wills and estate planning

James Beresford

Published by: Wilkinson Publishing Pty Ltd ACN 006 042 173

Level 4, 2 Collins Street, Melbourne, Vic 3000
Tel: 03 9654 5446, www.wilkinsonpublishing.com.au
Copyright © 2017 Slater and Gordon LLP. All rights reserved.

The Author

James is the National Practice Group Leader for the Wills, Tax, Trusts and Probate department at Slater and Gordon Lawyers. He is especially interested in helping people deal with their estate planning, where clear communication, practical skills and life experience are as critical as legal knowledge.

James also lectures to post-graduate students at a leading law university and for the Solicitors Group at conferences for law professionals. One of his great skills is taking a pragmatic approach to solving problems and by simplifying complex issues by using language that everyone can understand.

James is married and has a daughter and spends his time outside of work enjoying the West Yorkshire countryside.

For Claire and Sophie

Introduction

A client once said to me that he wanted to make his will to cover what would happen 'if he died'. Obviously, he knows something that I don't, because it is not a case of 'if' but 'when'.

My father has always told me that there are two guarantees in life: tax and death, both of which I will consider in this book.

Everybody needs a will. It's as simple as that. That's why this book is written for everybody.

I hope that this book will explain in simple terms the steps that are needed to prepare an effective will and other estate planning documents. Where relevant, I've listed options at various stages to help with your decision-making.

Much like my client above, most of us expect to live to a ripe old age but the reality is we could pass away at any time. So it's important to start planning before it's too late.

Lots of 'just-in-case' decisions need to be made now. For example, there could be a time in the future when you're still alive but can't make decisions for yourself. That day could be tomorrow.

Estate planning isn't all about death. It includes Lasting Powers of Attorney, which most people don't even think about. These involve appointing someone to make medical, financial or legal decisions on your behalf, in the event that you can't, either because of failing mental capacity, or because you're in a coma, after someone ran a red light. If you nominate your 'sister Sue' to make decisions for you, so be it. Otherwise it's up to the courts, and they may pick your 'big brother Bill' who you never liked and is the family 'black sheep'.

That's quite true of almost every area of this book — either make the decision yourself or it's out of your hands. You may hope that your friends or relations will carry out your wishes but there is no guarantee that your unwritten wishes will be carried out (it can be tough enough getting the written ones through!).

James Beresford
Wills, Tax, Trusts and Probate
Slater and Gordon Lawyers

Contents

I. Write a will

Write a will.

Do it now. It's no big deal, it won't hurt.

Sixty per cent of adults in the United Kingdom don't have one. Many of the remaining forty per cent are unaware that their existing will is inappropriate for their current circumstances and needs updating. They may have made the will sometime ago before they had children or before they had acquired wealth.

If you have no will, the distribution of your estate will be determined by the law and could result in your loved ones not receiving as much as you would like. It can also cause, in certain circumstances, the administration of your estate to be unnecessarily delayed. You won't get to choose who manages your estate, nor will you get to select who receives your property.

Your estate will be distributed in accordance with the rules of intestacy (a statutory formula). Your own wishes won't be taken into consideration because – remember – you left none.

Under the rules of intestacy, your spouse or civil partner may only be entitled to part of your estate, there may be no provision for your children, grandchildren or other relatives, a co-habitee will not benefit from your estate and there may be a larger inheritance tax bill than there needs to be.

A disappointed beneficiary may then bring a claim against your estate which will not only add to the time and cost of the administration, it may cause irreparable damage to the family dynamic. You will see that it's all a bit 'up in the air'. That's why everybody should write a will.

People say to me, 'James, I'm only 30 or 40, why should I bother with all this stuff now?' or 'I don't own much so why bother?'

As for the timing I invariably reply, 'because by the time you get around to doing it, it may be too late! In fact, you may procrastinate for so long that you never write one at all'. And on the issue of wealth, 'it's not only about wealth; a will covers other immediate issues you should address such as guardianship of children and your digital assets. Besides, if you do it now it's in place when you do accumulate enough assets to lose sleep over'.

Younger people don't bother to write a will because they associate dying with old age. They think (if they think about it at all) that writing a will is something someone does when approaching death, which is supposedly when you're older. A glance at the daily news reminds us that death doesn't respect age.

Even the loss of capacity, which is generally associated with aged care, can be an issue for young people; all it can take is a car accident or a collapsed rugby scrum.

Just as signing a Lasting Power of Attorney doesn't make you mentally incapable, signing a will won't kill you. At worst it's a paper cut, I promise you.

I recommend you make the decision to act now so you can do so without pressure and maximise the chances of making the right decision.

And look what happens when you don't write one!

ACTION Writing your will is your first step.

CASE STUDY

WHAT CAN HAPPEN WITHOUT A WILL

John lived with his partner Mary. They had lived together for one year prior to his death. They had one child together, Jack, who was one year old. John had been married before to Anna; whilst they had separated four years ago they had never got around to divorcing.

The house that Mary shared with John was in John's sole name and was worth £200,000. John's other assets included bank accounts in his name with a total balance of £60,000 and one joint bank account with Mary with a balance of £2,000.

John died in a car accident and had not made a will.

Under the rules of intestacy Mary will not receive any of his estate (although she will inherit the joint bank account by survivorship). Anna (as the surviving spouse – remember they never divorced) will receive the first £250,000 of the estate, John's personal chattels (household and personal goods) and half of the rest of the estate (£5,000). Jack will receive the remaining £5,000 when he attains the age of 18 years or if he marries earlier.

You will see that the division of the estate is unfair and could put Mary at risk of being homeless (the house would pass to Anna). Mary would then be able to leave her estate in due course to whoever she wants. The only way that Mary and Jack could increase the benefit they receive from the estate would be to bring a claim against the estate which would be both stressful and expensive.

INTESTACY LAWS

If you die without leaving a will in England and Wales, the intestacy laws come in to play. It then depends on your family tree who gets what when you die. The following table sets out the position succinctly however the main points to note are as follows:

Where there is no will and you are married or in a civil partnership, your spouse/civil partner (even if you are separated) will inherit your estate if it is less than £250,000. If you don't have children then your spouse will inherit all of your estate regardless of size.

The position becomes much more complicated if you have children and your estate is over £250,000. Here your spouse/civil partner will inherit the first £250,000, your personal chattels (household and personal goods) and half the remainder. Your children will inherit the remaining half in equal shares.

If you die without a spouse but with children then your children would inherit your estate equally between them even if you have a 'common law' spouse. If there are no children, then your estate will go to your parents, and from the parents down to other family members.

It is not uncommon for distant relatives to inherit parts of an estate where someone has not left a will. People who are related to you but have had no involvement in your life could benefit from your estate. Typically the phone call that we receive when such family members are told of their inheritance consists of two questions. Firstly, 'how much am I getting?' and secondly 'who is it that has died?'

Am I scaremongering or being a tad melodramatic? If only it were fantasy. Ever heard the saying that truth is stranger than fiction? Search around the internet for stories and court decisions about family hardship and disputes arising from the absence of a will or a 'proper' will. The reality is that living without a will is like playing Russian roulette with your estate.

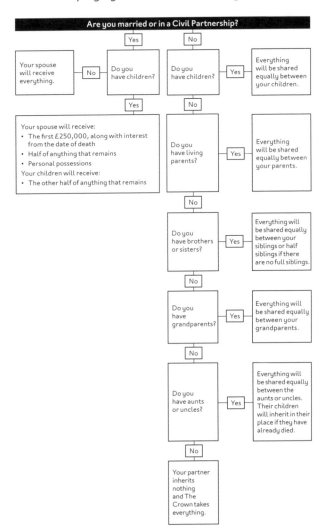

"No will – no say"

WHAT IS A WILL?

A will determines how your assets are to be divided in the event of your death. It's a formal document that enables you to pass assets from one generation to the next. A will must comply with strict legal requirements concerning both the form of the document and the way it's executed.

FORMAL REQUIREMENTS

Most lay people aren't aware of the formal legal requirements of completing a will, so they can very easily overlook them. Let me tell you a bit more about them to give you a better understanding.

The necessary formalities of a legal will are:
1. **Signature**,
2. **Date**,
3. A clear statement that it's the **final will**, i.e. an opening phrase such as: 'This is my last Will and Testament...' (In the absence of that, it might be nothing more than a jotting of what you might be contemplating at the time.)
4. **Two witnesses** who aren't beneficiaries. A lawyer need not be present.
5. **The willmaker and both witnesses** must all observe each other sign the document.

Some people literally pull out a sheet of paper, write 'when I die I want my assets to go to X', get two witnesses to sign and date it — and that's their will. Or so they hope.

All too often they get it wrong. The rules relating to wills and asset ownership can appear deceivingly simple, when the reality is they aren't.

OPTIONS

Some people use a do-it-yourself will kit (DIY). Something bought from their local Post Office or a high street shop. Others choose to use an equally inexpensive online template will.

Many people believe they're saving money choosing the cheapest options and that there's no real need to pay a lawyer to prepare a will. After all, aren't they very simple documents that anyone can prepare? You can be forgiven for thinking so, but you would be very wrong.

You'll discover during the course of reading this book that a professionally prepared will, where the complexities of the law and your individual assets are taken into account, doesn't cost much. In fact, relatively little when the cost of making an error is factored in.

A lot of people use a template will. They fill it in themselves and hope for the best. Those types of wills are sometimes enough. It's true that they do address many general needs. But whether they do or don't satisfy a particular individual's needs is very much a roll of the dice. Because if it does, it means their affairs are extremely simple and they don't need any bells or whistles. The problem with do-it-yourself wills is the complications in affairs that require special attention that they aren't aware of.

The danger of doing it yourself is you don't know whether the simple will covers everything, or whether you need something more. The point is: **lay people don't know what they don't know.**

RECOMMENDATION

Have your personal requirements assessed before you jump in the deep end. Speak with a lawyer – it won't hurt. You will at least know what issues have to be addressed, even if you don't have all the answers.

COMPLICATIONS

Individuals may have complications within their personal or financial affairs that require special advice and special treatment. Complications they often don't realise exist, or if they do, they might not know the options available to deal with them.

Examples of complications requiring special attention:
- A blended family.
- A family trust.
- They've separated from a spouse and not yet divorced.
- Their estate includes royalties or patents.
- Step-children or other non-relatives who are (or claim to be) dependents.
- Property they wish to pass to A which would otherwise automatically go to B, a joint owner.
- Shareholding in family companies.
- A whole range of things that people overlook because they don't know that these things are relevant.

"No will – no say"

Some of those issues will be easy to address. Others will be more complex.

Relationship breakdowns invariably complicate people's lives. These issues can certainly affect a will.

COST

Compared to other legal procedures, the cost of having a will prepared is relatively inexpensive.

Slater and Gordon, a large law firm with a reputation for quality service, charges as little as £150 for its lawyer assisted will, and £250 for a standard will prepared in the traditional way. In the event that you have something more sophisticated than a standard will, the next level of will – one with trust arrangements – is £600. A local lawyer would charge a similar price.

Wouldn't you invest that sort of money for the peace of mind it can provide knowing it's been done properly?

There are of course more expensive estate planning packages available for those who have very complex personal or financial affairs but they form a small part of our community.

BUT WHY PAY I HEAR YOU ASK?

You might ask 'why pay when I can do an unassisted DIY will, get it done for free or maybe pay just a nominal sum?'

Let me share a word of caution. The value and true worth of a properly prepared will has been undermined and people have been misled into believing that they're 'such simple documents' that anyone can prepare a will. The formal legal requirements, the high chance of making an error and the dire consequences of getting it wrong have evaporated in the minds of many. Like a sharp knife in the hands of a child, all may be OK, but there is plenty of scope for disaster.

Who is responsible for creating this misconception? We lawyers and will writers have to shoulder most of the blame.

As lawyers have a long-term relationship with their clients (i.e. the family lawyer), preparing wills has been historically treated as a bit of a freebie or as a loss-leader to maintain the relationship knowing that in the long term the investment of their time will pay dividends. Some might see this as good business sense and a good service offering to clients, but it does have the side effect of leading people to believe that wills are easy and simple because lawyers barely charge anything for them.

There are two consequences of these practices:
- Lawyers lose money preparing wills.
- By undercharging, lawyers have contributed to the devaluing of the importance and complexity of wills in the minds of the public.

The result? The public is given the impression that, 'wills are so simple lawyers even give them away, so I should be able to do one myself or at the very least buy a cheap one anywhere'. That's a general mindset that lawyers are partly responsible for creating. It's wrong and dangerous.

Another consequence of lawyers undertaking cheap or free wills as a loss-lead is this: how much time would you think that a lawyer will spend understanding their client's needs and addressing them meaningfully? As time is money, lawyers and will writers have been known to take as little time as possible.

As they're losing money on the transaction, there is a risk that lawyers and will writers will get the client in, get the basic instructions, write a basic will, and then get them out. Time is money. Whether the will is appropriate may be another thing all together.

There are some exceptions, for example, preparing free wills for member organisations (e.g. unions or charities) where the lawyer enjoys a commercial benefit from dealing with the organisation. It's in their commercial interest to spend time on the file to ensure the organisation's members are properly attended to.

Without proper advice, you may well end up with a standard will that doesn't take into account your individual family and financial circumstances. This could be quite dangerous for the future of your estate. Don't get me wrong, many standard wills are perfectly fine. The ones that cause problems are those where complications are overlooked because of lack of thorough investigation and this takes time and costs money.

There are simply no free lunches and you get what you pay for. Nothing more, but sometimes, a lot less.

THE CASE (CURSE) OF THE HOMEMADE WILL

A couple once came to see me, let's call them Peter and Susan. Peter's father, Jack, had died some years ago and left his estate to his second wife Jean. Jack and Jean married later on in life and Jack, in his will, left his estate to Jean.

After Jack's death, Jean visited her solicitor to prepare a will in which she appointed Peter as the executor, left the house (which had been Jack's) to Peter, various cash gifts to charities and then the remainder to Peter and Susan equally.

She then wanted to change her will and Peter contacted the solicitor and upon hearing the cost to change the will (£200 plus VAT) Peter decided that it was too expensive and took matters into his own hands because wills are 'simple'.

Using the original will as a starting point, Peter amended it by adding in clauses he found on the internet and deleting clauses he deemed to be superfluous.

After Jean's death, I sat with Peter and Susan and explained to them the provisions of the homemade will. Peter was still named as the executor, the gift of the house was still included but the house had been sold and therefore was not owned at the date of death. That gift therefore failed. A professionally drawn will would have included provision for a replacement property or a gift of the proceeds of sale instead. This will had neither. The charitable legacies remained untouched (thankfully). For some reason Peter had deleted the residuary clause which left the balance to him and his wife equally. This meant that the estate (save for the legacies to charity) would be divided in accordance with the rules of intestacy.

Peter was never adopted by Jean (he was an adult when she met his father) therefore he would not benefit under the intestacy. He was not financially dependent on her so could not bring a claim against the estate.

The value of the estate that should have passed to him was £260,000. He was however the executor so he had to deal with the administration of the estate whilst remote relatives of Jean who had little or no contact with her received the estate.

By trying to save £240 it cost him £260,000 – a costly mistake.

SIMPLE NEEDS OR MORE COMPLEX – WHICH CATEGORY DO YOU FALL INTO?

Answer: You probably need to be an experienced wills and probate lawyer to make that call.

SAFE KEEPING

The decision where to store a will, once signed, rests with you, the individual client. It's up to you to determine what you want to do with it. Some clients want to take it home; others want to deposit it with the bank.

Most lawyers will offer to store the will and other documents (like title deeds) in safe custody at no cost.

IS THERE ANYTHING WRONG WITH THIS PRACTICE?

No, it provides the client certainty and security for their documents but more than that it increases the chances that their executor will engage the client's preferred lawyer to look after their family's interests during the probate and estate administration process. It makes good sense for all concerned. It also assists the family expedite the probate application when that time comes.

HOW OFTEN DO YOU NEED TO REVIEW YOUR WILL?

Answer: You should review it every time there's a major change in your financial or family life.

There are some life events that automatically affect your will:
- Marriage or re-marriage invalidates an existing will, unless it expressly states that it was drafted with that marriage in mind.
- Divorce automatically excludes your former spouse from your will but only on issue of the decree absolute.

Other life events could include an acquisition or a disposal of an asset or business. It could be a birth, a death or a marriage of someone affected by your will. It could also be a separation from a common law partner or embarking on a new relationship. When a big event like that happens, you should revisit the will, think about it and ask, 'have I already covered that event as a contingency in the will? If not – perhaps I should amend it'. If you can't work that out, ask a lawyer.

In 9/10 cases the answer will be 'no you don't have to amend the will because it already takes into account that situation'. But occasionally, a paragraph may need re-working to bring it up-to-date.

There are some circumstances though where you'll completely need to **redo your will**.

1st Will: A person might write their first will in their 20s or 30s – with a partner, no children and a property with a mortgage.

2nd will: By 40 they've got children, small investments, a mortgage and other debts.

3rd will: By 50 one of their children might be in a failing marriage, another in a high risk business, and the third with a disability – who struggles to handle money. Their future inheritance is at risk and a simple will won't help.

4th will: By 65 they find they've made a reasonable amount of money over time, with a paid-up mortgage, family trust, investment property and perhaps superannuation and life policies. The risks previously identified become even bigger in magnitude. Managing the estate will be much more complex as many of the assets may bypass the estate and require separate management (such as superannuation death benefits, insurance proceeds, trust assets and interest in jointly owned assets).

Managing all the issues that flow from those things requires a bespoke (individually crafted) will and estate planning, designed to address those specific circumstances.

Again the will should be reviewed whenever there's a major change.

ACTION   As a catch-all, even in the absence of a major event, I recommend that people should review their will once every three years.

I didn't say re-write or revamp. I simply suggest pulling it out every three years, re-reading it, thinking about it and simply checking that it all still makes sense in your current circumstances.

Unless you live a turbulent life, most times you'll say, 'that's still okay...' and slip it back into your sock drawer. If not, ask your lawyer.

FACTORS TO CONSIDER

An estate is usually composed of physical belongings (such as cash, clothes, jewellery, cars and the family home) as well as investments such as a share portfolio and nowadays even digital assets such as photos and documents stored on a computer or in the cloud.

The **protection of inheritances** is one important factor to consider. If a beneficiary faces:
- A failed marriage (almost 42 per cent of marriages fail).
- Remarriage.
- Bankruptcy.
- Loss of mental capacity.
- Drug, alcohol or gambling dependency.
- Spending problems, or
- Family disputes.

What happens to their inheritance when they receive it?

Does part or even all of your hard-earned wealth end up in the hands of a child's ex-spouse, their creditors or their book-keepers?

A second consideration is the **minimisation of the inheritance tax** burden for your estate and your beneficiaries, once they take ownership of your property.

A third, important consideration is deciding upon **guardians** to care for your children if they're still minors when you pass away. Assuming it will be their godparents or step-parent would be wrong. You formally need to nominate someone and you can do so in your will.

Preparing a will is a part of the bigger picture of preparing a succession plan. But is it all about death?

Definitely not. Succession planning is also about the here and now, as much as it's about what happens when you pass away. To protect your family and your property you should take into account problems that you, or they, may face during your lifetime. Failing health, accidents, financial management, insurance needs, debt management, business succession, investment planning, wealth accumulation for retirement and aged care are just a few of the issues that a comprehensive succession plan can and should address.

The legal components of succession planning should only be part of your broader succession planning strategy. A well thought-out succession plan should include legal documents that are coordinated with your retirement, investment and wealth accumulation strategies. It often requires a coordinated and cooperative approach to a client's planning by their lawyer, accountant, insurance adviser and investment adviser. Professionals operating independently of each other can (and often does) result in chaos. Legal, financial and personal affairs resembling a bowl of tangled spaghetti isn't the ideal structured pathway to the future.

A structured strategy and proper documentation will ensure that all parties are on the same page at each stage of your life journey – from now to death and beyond. A good plan is capable of being followed as the years roll on. A specialist lawyer can work in tandem with your accountant, financial planner and insurance adviser. Doing this provides security and certainty for you and your family. Spending time and money now on the right professional advice will save you and your family heartache in the future.

EXECUTOR

Choosing the right executor is as important as choosing your Guardian and Attorney. An executor's job isn't for the faint-hearted. Ask anyone who has taken on that role; they'll tell you that the duties can be difficult, stressful and time consuming. These responsibilities include applying for probate and administering and distributing your estate. In some cases (too many) it may also involve fending off attacks on the estate by wannabe beneficiaries.

When weighing up your potential executor, make sure you choose a capable, trustworthy person. You don't need a professional person to act as executor (for example, a lawyer) but sometimes it's a great advantage. Any person with mental capacity and over the age of 18 years can be appointed. This includes your children and beneficiaries. Yes, your children can be appointed as executors, but are unable to act until they're 18 years of age.

Whoever is appointed will have to be on hand when his or her services are required. As a rule of thumb, I suggest you avoid appointing elderly people or those who live far away.

Whom you choose will depend on:
- **Complexity**. The complexity of your financial and family affairs.
- **Skills**. The skills of the potential candidates.
- **Negotiating skills**. The likelihood the executor will have to deal with disputes over the estate.
- **Impartiality**. Whether or not the executor will have a conflict of interest. If they manage the estate and are also a beneficiary, others in the family may perceive favouritism. If they don't get on in any way, sharing the role of executor can almost guarantee disputes.

The most common choices are:
- Wife, husband, partner or children.
- Friend or business partner.
- Professional adviser – possibly a lawyer, accountant or both.
- A trust corporation.

It's preferable to have more than one executor and/or a substitute executor in case one executor dies, is unable to act, or starts to act but can't continue to do so. Alternatively, you can nominate a firm of lawyers, a trustee corporation or a bank, but it's important that you enquire about their fees and charges beforehand.

The executor is required to gather all the assets, secure them, pay existing debts and then distribute assets in accordance with the terms of the will.

Estate administration refers to the process that the executor of an estate goes through to manage and distribute the estate assets in accordance with the terms of the will.

2. Start planning now

Estate Planning is like planning a trip to visit a friend who has moved house.

Sometimes it's simple and other times it's more complex, depending on where they have moved:
- Around the corner – minimum planning needed.
- To the other side of town that you're not familiar with – before setting off check the address, how to get there and how long it will take.
- To a new city you're not familiar with – same as the other side of town but the travel logistics will require a lot more planning.
- To a new country – same as a new city but with added planning, attention to timing, cost of travel, transport to and from airports and the time away from home.

The complexity of each plan varies, but the time to do the planning in each case is before you leave home. It's too late to think about getting a passport when you arrive at the airport.

In other words, the time to plan is now. Your journey through life has already begun and if you haven't got your plan already in place, you need to do so before you meet any unexpected barrier to your progress.

NON ESTATE ASSETS

You may hold **investments** in your own name, through a company, a pension fund or through a trust.

If you own assets personally, when you die your executor gathers the assets together and takes control of them. The executor holds them on trust until your debts are paid and then distributes the assets in accordance with your will.

Whilst in the executor's control these assets are referred to as a person's deceased estate. But not all assets you control are actually owned by you personally and therefore may not become part of your estate.

For example, your pension death benefit may go directly to your spouse, as might your life insurance proceeds or your half-share of a jointly owned property. These items often go direct to a person without ever becoming part of your estate. That is, they bypass your estate and aren't controlled by your will.

If you are a beneficiary of a trust that owns investments or other assets, the trust will continue to own those assets after you pass away. In order to ensure the trust and its assets pass to your desired successor you need to know who will inherit control of your trust and how. This requires a close examination of the terms of the trust deed and often requires documents to be prepared in tandem to your will. I explain this further a little later in this chapter.

You can, however, make relatively minor changes to the way you manage these assets so that they go into your estate or are controlled by the terms of your will.

Questions:
1. Do I have any assets that won't form part of my estate and are therefore outside the control of my will?
2. Is my current situation the best arrangement for my dependants and me or should I change my arrangements so my will controls these assets?
3. Can I change my current arrangements so that one or more of these assets is controlled by my will?

Consider:
- Assets held in a family trust don't form part of your estate. They can't be directly dealt with by your will.
- Other assets may or may not pass through your estate, depending on whether you want them to or not. For example, pension death benefits, life insurance proceeds and interests in jointly owned property (if owned as joint tenants). You have to determine whether they go through your estate or bypass your estate and go directly to another person. You have to know the current situation with these assets and make changes if required to satisfy your wishes. For example, a joint tenancy on a property can be 'severed' so that you own the property as 'tenants in common' which means that your half of the property can pass under the terms of your will to your desired beneficiary.

The complexities don't enable me to elaborate on all of these options and variables in this book. If you don't know the pros and cons of each option, don't guess, the outcome could be the opposite of what you want. Below are some important insights into a few of the more common issues you may face.

A LITTLE MORE ABOUT TRUSTS

Trusts are complicated things (as you will see later!), the workings of which are little understood by many people who have them. Putting aside the technical legal issues of legal and beneficial ownership and the role of a trustee – in effect **a trust owns assets and holds them on behalf of beneficiaries**. You can't pass on these assets in your will – as you don't own them (the trust owns them).

Selecting the best option in your particular circumstances is a planning issue for you to address.

Again, ignoring the technical legal structure of a trust, **a trust** is in effect a legal entity in its own right. Someone has to manage it – the trustee. Quite often a professional (such as a lawyer or an investment company) looks after the day-to-day control of the assets. It might be a share portfolio or properties, and the beneficiary is 'all family members'.

It is the trust deed that sets out who is to benefit from the trust and not your will. There may be options available to you during your life to ensure that your chosen beneficiary (if possible) benefits from trust assets on your death.

The takeaway message here is to think about what you wish to happen and take the appropriate advice. No bonus points for guessing that a free or cheap will won't address these issues.

The starting point in every case is to **read the trust deed** and understand how it works.

PROTECTING BENEFICIARIES FROM THEMSELVES

Every family has a cross to bear. Whether it's a dysfunctional child, a family member with some kind of addiction (i.e. alcohol, drugs, online shopping or gambling), a spendthrift, a poor money manager, someone who's manipulated by their partner or a child with a disability. The outcome is the same – emotional and financial stress surrounding the planning process.

Parents have come to me with concerns that a family member is likely to squander the inheritance they'd like to leave them. Sometimes they want to cut them out entirely as the inheritance will only make existing problems worse. On occasions it's tempting to agree. However, there may be options that fall between the two extremes of leaving money with no strings attached and leaving nothing.

If you're concerned that any inheritance you leave your offspring might be wasted away, here are a few ideas to consider:

1. Place the inheritance in a trust

If you doubt your child will make sound decisions about spending their inheritance you can put those decisions in the hands of someone else. You can leave the money in a trust and appoint a competent person to manage the funds for the benefit of your child.

Your child will get the benefit of using assets in the trust and perhaps enjoy the benefits of an income stream. But they never get to spend (or squander) the capital.

These types of arrangements are many and varied so can be tailored to suit your particular circumstances.

2. Instalments and annuities

People sometimes grow out of their shortcomings. If you're hopeful that maturity will bring a change of their behaviour, you can prepare a will that staggers the inheritance payments. For example, one-third at age 25, another third at age 35 and the balance at age 40.

Alternatively, you could establish an annuity (a contract with an insurance company that obligates the company to make payments to a beneficiary). Annuities are often used to provide retirement income, but you can also direct payments to a child. You can arrange either for regular payments of a set amount for a certain period of time or you can arrange for variable payments that depend on the size of the investment premium.

Again the structures are flexible and can be tailored to fit.

PERSONAL EFFECTS

Big disputes are often caused by small items of little financial value. Items of sentimental value, such as memorabilia, photographs or 'Dad's favourite watch' are often not specifically gifted to an individual by the will.

I once had two siblings litigate over control of their mother's estate (they were both executors and the only beneficiaries) because they couldn't agree on who would receive one small item of furniture which had negligible commercial value but lots of sentimental value. They spent their inheritance fighting each other in the courts; neither wanted the other to get anything from the estate. Their dislike of each other escalated at about the same rate as the legal fees climbed. Or perhaps, more likely, it happened the other way round – sibling rivalry and associated high emotion make volatile fuel to feed ugly disputes.

To avoid this, some people choose to write out a list in their will that says, 'Johnny's having that and Mary's having that...' and they go through everything in the house. That's one way of doing it, and the most legally enforceable. It can also result in our more senior clients continuously changing their wills as family members fall in and out of favour, or as items are broken or thrown out.

A compromise is to make mention in your will that if you leave a list of gifts, you wish your executors to do their best to distribute the gifts in accordance with that list. It's not binding on the executors (as a list in the will would be) but it does give the executors formal guidance and authority to deal with the listed items. *That way the list can be updated as often as required without having to formally rewrite the will.* This option however doesn't overcome sibling rivalry if they're also the executors.

In cases where people have been partnered for long enough to have acquired most of their things together, these items are treated as being jointly owned unless there is some reason to attribute ownership to one or the other. So when one partner dies the surviving partner automatically owns it all, without going through the will. Generally speaking, that's what happens.

There are some exceptions though. Sometimes it's really 'mine' not 'ours'. For example, where someone has a hobby in which their partner has no interest. In my case it's football and cricket... but let's suppose it's golf. Technically speaking it might be difficult or impossible to establish whether these items are legally owned by the golfer alone or jointly owned with the non-golfing partner.

It's common however, for such items to be treated by partners as being owned by one or the other, regardless of how they were acquired. Quite often a person will leave such items to a particular person (usually a son/daughter, niece/nephew or friend) who shares that interest. A mother will often leave her jewellery to one (or more) of her daughters and will actually specify who gets which item. And a father will traditionally leave his vintage car that needs restoring to one of his sons.

People who are preparing their will should consider, 'what's the value of those items of memorabilia in the beneficiary's hands?' If it only has sentimental value, that's fine. But if it's an item that has some commercial value then it may need extra consideration.

Suppose it's something that can be published, like a war diary. Such an item has sentimental value, but also a potentially added value as a published book. In the hands of the beneficiary it's much more valuable than your collection of detective novels that someone else receives. It's your choice to ignore the actual value of items, and many do... **But**: make it a conscious decision by thinking through these issues and addressing fairness, if required, to balance things up.

Also, if the item is valuable ask yourself; is it to be treated as part of a child's share of the balance of the estate or is it to be treated as a gift which is in addition to their equal share of the balance of the estate?

Fairness doesn't necessarily mean equal value, but what you view as fair may be seen as unfair by your beneficiaries – **so talk to them about it before you leave behind a ticking time bomb**. Explain your reasoning; it could (and most often does) avoid a family feud once you leave the scene.

WHAT DOES 'EQUAL' MEAN?

In the situation where the first partner dies, the administration of their will usually progresses reasonably smoothly. This is because the deceased usually leaves everything to the other partner, who now has a houseful of furniture, memorabilia, trinkets, knick-knacks, etc. Of course, that may upset some relatives such as the survivor's step-children (the deceased children by an earlier partner), but generally people don't like to disrupt an existing household.

But don't assume things will be smooth sailing. In these circumstances step-children often feel vulnerable as they feel their inheritance is disappearing into the coffers of their step-parent. There are numerous legal strategies you can implement to protect their future inheritance once their step-parent passes away.

MUTUAL WILLS

One such strategy is the use of Mutual Wills.

Couples often wish to leave their estate to each other and then, on the death of the survivor, have their combined estate divided between their respective families. Typically this occurs with blended families where there are children from prior relationships.

Each party relies on the survivor to 'do the right thing'.

Generally, there are no restrictions on a person changing their will. When the first passes away, the surviving partner can alter their will. This may result in a new will that does not reflect their current shared intentions. For example, the surviving partner may alter their will to remove step-children as beneficiaries and to favour their own children or a new life partner. With all the best intentions, circumstances change and it is impossible to predict what might happen in the future, particularly if the surviving partner is under the influence of third parties.

How do you ensure that your property ends up in the hands of your preferred beneficiaries, whilst allowing your partner to have use of your assets whilst they are still alive?

There is no single or simple solution.

One estate planning tool designed to help minimise this type of risk is an agreement you enter into with your partner to the effect that neither of you will change the broad intentions in your will after the first dies. You can make Mutual Wills.

Mutual Wills serve as a mechanism to reduce the chances of the surviving partner changing their mind with respect to their will.

On the first death, a trust is established over the deceased spouse's estate at that date and whilst the survivor can if he/she wants change his/her will it cannot dispose of the assets in the trust.

Therefore, Mutual Wills give rise to obligations on the part of the surviving partner. The surviving partner becomes the trustee of the estate for the beneficiaries named in the wills. The surviving partner is bound by the agreement.

If either partner changes their will contrary to the agreement, the courts may intervene to enforce the agreement.

Breaches and remedies: It is important that the beneficiaries are informed of the existence of the agreement, as they have the right to enforce the agreement. If the surviving partner has unreasonably exhausted all the assets of the deceased, beneficiaries may sue for breach of contract.

Shortcomings of Mutual Wills:

1. Mutual Wills cannot prevent the estate from being challenged.

2. Changes in circumstances may occur after the Mutual Wills have been executed which may result in the survivor being disadvantaged. A remarriage of the surviving partner can also complicate the operation of the agreement.

3. The survivor may deliberately attempt to frustrate the operation of Mutual Wills by depleting estate assets or changing the way they are owned.

Remarriage: It is important to note that remarriage will not change the obligations under the agreement but remarriage will automatically terminate an existing will. The survivor should see a solicitor to obtain advice should they remarry.

Conclusion: Mutual Wills can be one 'tool' you can use to achieve your wishes. They could be a solution but they are imperfect and do not guarantee protection.

There are other strategies that can be used as an alternate to Mutual Wills to help preserve your testamentary intentions.

Problems usually occur when the second partner dies. This is because a lot more people can dispute the will. In many instances, the parents simply leave instructions to 'divide my estate equally'. But unless there's some description of what 'equally' means, that's almost asking for trouble because (to make sense of the estate) the executor must ask the question: 'what does *equal* mean?'

→ Does that mean equal **financial value**? (Should we have every item valued?)
→ Does it mean equal in **number** of items? (If I get one, you get one.)
→ And when you've worked that out, ask – does a cutlery set count as one item? Or is each individual piece a single item?
→ Or, does it refer to equal **sentimental value**? (How do we measure that?)

If you don't want to specify which item goes to whom, you could write something like this into the will: 'I leave all my goods and chattels to my three children. The eldest can choose the first item; the second child has second choice; the third child has third choice... (and a set of anything is to be treated as a single item!)' and so they continue in that rotation.

Or, you could do what my grandmother did (and I'm sure lots of other grandmothers did too!). She stuck coloured stickers on the back of each item on which she wrote the initials of the person whom she wanted to receive it. The notes had no legal effect but at least her executors had some guide as to who should get what. Although I've always wondered if someone may have swapped a few stickers around.

I wouldn't recommend my grandmother's approach, but more than one granny has ignored my advice in the past and I'm sure others will choose to do so in the future.

DIGITAL ASSETS

With the Computer Age there comes a new type of asset – digital assets.

Digital assets are defined in the USA as 'an electronic record in which an individual has a right or interest. The term does not include an underlying asset of liability unless the asset or liability is itself an electronic record'. I appreciate that this definition lends itself to lawyers but common types of digital assets include (to name but a few):
- Photos stored online.
- Blogs.
- Bitcoins and the like.
- eBooks.
- Social media.
- Online gaming avatars.

What digital assets do you own? For example, do you own your online digital library? No you don't. What about all the photographs on Facebook, Flickr or that type of service provider? In most cases their *Terms and Conditions* will say they own it. But few people read the terms and conditions, and even fewer understand them. Once the service provider knows you've died, many will cut off access to your account and close it whilst others offer other options if you authorise your executor to deal with them on your behalf.

This is a rapidly changing area however as the public demands more control. Governments in some countries are legislating to allow executors greater rights over a deceased person's digital assets.

Question: Memorialised? What's that?

Answer: When you die, the website manager (service provider) leaves your online content 'up there' and freezes the account, therefore confirmed friends can look at it in the future for a specific period of time or perhaps forever. The site can't be accessed by the general public however.

Some websites, such as Facebook, allow pages to be memorialised in a way that enables family and friends ('confirmed friends') to access the account and add new posts and photographs to the account, in memory of the deceased.

Each service provider's terms and conditions differ, and they're continuously changing. It's worth checking your status, as your digital assets may or may not be part of your estate that can be managed by your executor. But remember, even if your account managers don't currently play ball, their policies are changing as rapidly as technology itself.

RECOMMENDATION

Catalogue your digital assets and access codes, store in a safe place (with your will perhaps) and instruct your executor or attorney what you want done with them. If you need help, just ask me or one of my colleagues at Slater and Gordon.

OTHER 'VIRTUAL' ISSUES

It's important your executor is made aware of all your accounts so they can be dealt with. Executors often haven't undertaken the role before and aren't aware of the duties and obligations imposed on them by the law, so don't keep these details a secret – unless of course there is good reason to do so.

LinkedIn will stop 'Invitations to Follow' a person once advised that the person has passed away. But someone with authority has to ask and provide evidence of death. I recently met a chap who still gets invitations to follow his best friend who died two years ago. It upsets him every time the invitation appears, but he has no authority to put a stop to it occurring.

As for bank accounts, betting accounts, shopping accounts and the like, I'd recommend all details be removed from a deceased person's accounts ASAP. There is the risk of being hacked and no one noticing it. But that's not the only problem. Too many of us, myself included, ask our internet browsers to 'remember' our passwords. Add that to the fact that our login ID is often easy to guess (our email address or another obvious identifier) and anyone can access our accounts and have a spending spree by simply turning on our computer, tablet or smartphone. Abuse of an account-linked credit card will eventually come to the notice of an executor, but as they say... by that stage the horse has bolted.

BEGINNING THE PLANNING DISCUSSION

Most people feel somewhat uncomfortable discussing their own mortality with members of their family. Death is a taboo topic for many, but it's not just death and the division of property after someone dies that is neglected.

Unless discussed and planned for, there is no certainty about what happens if, through accident or the ageing process, a person loses the ability to look after his/her own personal, legal and financial affairs. *That's why these things should be discussed* and planned as soon as possible. Remember the passport example?

Death and loss of mental capacity aren't the exclusive domain of the elderly. People of all ages die or lose capacity every day. We don't control the timing of accidents, illness or our passing. The day will come when we'll no longer be capable of providing for the people we love, even if we can still care for ourselves. The consequences of these events are too important to leave to chance. It's even worth putting funeral arrangements in place in advance, to save your grieving family the burden of organising a funeral and burial/cremation when you pass away.

Fortunately, you can plan for that time and put structures in place now to help secure your future and that of your family. A well-structured plan can give great peace of mind that your loved ones will be provided for as you intended.

A **checklist of succession planning issues** you might consider and (as appropriate) discuss with family members, or your professional advisers can be found in **Schedule I** (page 65) of this book.

A good lawyer should have extensive experience across all or most of these areas and understand the complexities involved. S/he can help assess your personal circumstances, assist you to write an appropriate succession plan and work cooperatively with your other professional advisers such as your accountant and independent financial adviser to cover off on issues that are beyond a lawyer's professional discipline.

Appointing such a lawyer ensures that you will have an integrated plan that covers all the bases. And it needn't stop there. A good lawyer can help ensure that your dependants are looked after through whatever circumstances should arise over their lifetime.

The objectives of family succession planning are usually:

1. **Ongoing financial support of**
   - Spouse.
   - Children or other relatives.
   - Other dependants or organisations you support.
2. **Accumulation of wealth for**
   - Lifestyle needs.
   - Retirement.
3. **Structures for asset protection against**
   - Business risks.
   - Family risks.
4. **Continued control if you lose capacity**
   - Property and financial affairs attorney.
   - Health and welfare attorney.
5. **Coordinated strategies for asset distribution**
   - Business assets: company/partnership.
   - Trust assets: pension lump sum payments, life insurance.
   - Personal assets.
   - Digital assets.

Succession planning is a three-part process involving:
1. **Identification of assets.**
2. **Identification of potential risks.**
3. **Design and implementation of a succession plan taking into account items 1 and 2.**

Refer to Schedule 2 (page 68) of the book for a more comprehensive outline of this process.

WHERE DO YOU BEGIN THE PLANNING JOURNEY?

Let's begin now... I promise it won't hurt.

Questions: Are your succession planning needs straightforward? Do you have family or financial circumstances that require special attention? Do you know where to start? Do you have someone you can turn to for assistance? What will it involve?

Most people avoid succession planning because it's all too daunting. They simply don't know where to begin. Let's see if I can give you a head start.

Answer these questions 'yes' or 'no'.
- Do any beneficiaries suffer from a disability or have special needs?
- Do any beneficiaries have problems managing money?
- Do you have a blended family (children from a prior relationship)?
- Are any beneficiaries facing potential bankruptcy?
- Are any beneficiaries facing a potential relationship breakdown or divorce?
- Do any beneficiaries have an addiction problem (such as alcohol, gambling or drugs)?
- Do you wish to create a life interest in property or make a gift conditional?
- Are you a beneficiary of a trust?
- Do you own a business?
- Do you wish to leave a child out of your will?
- Have you any unresolved family law, property or maintenance issues?
- Do you have overseas assets or non-resident beneficiaries?

If you answered 'no' to these questions, your planning requirements are relatively straightforward and you should proceed to make a will with a Property and Financial affairs Lasting Power of Attorney and a Health and Welfare Lasting Power of Attorney without delay.

If you answered 'yes' to any of these questions, then you have identified an issue requiring specific attention. The longer you leave these matters, the harder it can be to address them in your plans. If you answer 'yes' to any of the questions concerning asset protection, or vulnerable beneficiaries then you'd be wise to include Chapter 5 and 6 in your perusal of this book.

Regardless of your answers, by undertaking this short exercise you have already begun the planning process, as you have identified any issues that require special attention so that you can seek the appropriate guidance.

Congratulations!

Now, take the next step and complete the Estate Planning Self-Assessment questionnaire in **Schedule 3** (page 70) of this book. It won't provide you with answers but may help you identify issues you need to address.

PROFESSIONAL GUIDANCE

Depending on your affairs, succession planning may not be complicated, but you can't be expected to know what you don't know.

Most people need some professional guidance to piece together their affairs. Some need a lot.

One of the most difficult things to achieve is choosing appropriate professional advisers to do the job. As mentioned before, that job is often a multidisciplinary task involving a lawyer, accountant and an independent financial adviser (IFA) or wealth manager. They will combine to identify and coordinate your legal needs along with asset protection, wealth accumulation, taxation advice, retirement planning and end of life matters. Most importantly, good advice is tailored to what matters most to you.

ACTION

When choosing a professional:
1. **Check** your adviser's experience, qualifications and reputation. For lawyers ask if they are members of the Society of Trust and Estate Practitioners (STEP), Solicitors for the Elderly or the Law Society's Wills and Inheritance Quality Scheme and for IFAs the Society of Later Life Advisers.
2. Get a **comprehensive breakdown** of what's included in the service and what isn't.
3. **Familiarise yourself** in advance with the issues you need to address and evaluate your adviser on how s/he addresses each of these (the questionnaire in Schedule 3 referred to above will be of great assistance here).
4. Find out upfront how **fees** are calculated.
5. Ensure your lawyer, financial planner, accountant and other advisers are happy to work together **cooperatively – this is extremely important**. If any of them are hesitant to deal with the others, replace the uncooperative one – s/he doesn't have your best interests at heart.

ACTION

The single most valuable piece of advice anyone can give you – *start planning today*, it's never too early. To find out more, and to contact your local Slater and Gordon Wills, Tax, Trusts and Probate lawyers, please call 0800 049 2824.

3. Inheritance tax

Inheritance tax (IHT) is a divisive tax and many people have strong opinions about it. People find it unfair that effectively someone's assets are taxed twice, once in life and then on death. I don't propose to offer my opinion on IHT, but to give you an overview of it and then I will provide details of certain exemptions that are available. This is meant to be a general overview of IHT and it is not intended to provide specific legal advice. As with all of these topics if you think that your estate may be liable for IHT then you need to speak to a professional to get the appropriate advice.

WHAT IS IHT?

IHT is a tax triggered both on death and in lifetime. Basically all transfers of value made by somebody are chargeable to IHT unless they come under one of the exemptions detailed below.

We each have our own Nil Rate Band (NRB) for IHT, this is currently (2016/17 tax year) £325,000 per person. Married couples and civil partners can utilise each other's NRB, this is called the Transferable Nil Rate Band (TNRB) and put simply the survivor can utilise any unused NRB of the first of the couple to die. In effect this means that married couples and civil partners have a combined NRB of (currently) £650,000. However as with everything, the TNRB is not as simple as you may think and you should seek the appropriate advice.

IHT is charged at three rates:
- 40 per cent – this is the death rate, in so far as if your estate exceeds your remaining NRB (or for a married couple the TNRB) the excess will be taxed at this rate.
- 20 per cent – this is the lifetime rate. If you make a Lifetime Chargeable Transfer (such as establishing a trust) (LCT) and the value of the LCT exceeds your NRB then excess will be charged at 20%. If you were to die within 7 years of the LCT then it will be reassessed for IHT. At this stage you will need to take appropriate professional advice.
- 36 per cent – If you leave 10 per cent of your net estate to charity a reduced rate of 36 per cent is available for the taxable part of the estate.

IHT EXEMPTIONS

It is possible to legitimately reduce the value of your estate during your lifetime to reduce the impact of IHT on your estate. This is not tax avoidance (which is bad) but effective legal estate planning.

You can make absolute gifts of any value during your lifetime and these will be excluded from your estate for IHT purposes if you survive 7 years from the date of the gift. If you fail to survive that period then the gifts will be caught and the value of the gift will reduce the NRB available on death or if the value of the gift exceeds the remaining NRB then IHT would be payable. These are called 'potentially exempt transfers'. You cannot retain any interest in the gifted property.

If you set up a trust in your lifetime then IHT may be chargeable at the lifetime rate (see above) if the value of the gift exceeds your NRB. These are known as 'lifetime chargeable transfers'.

LIFETIME EXEMPTIONS

Annual Exemption: We all have an annual exemption for IHT. This is currently £3,000 per annum and it is applied each financial (tax) year. In the first year that the annual exemption is used, you are allowed to use the previous year's exemption. In effect therefore, a couple could give away £12,000 in the first year without any IHT implications.

Example

John and Sue are a married couple and they have never contemplated estate planning. They decide to make a gift of £12,000 to their son James in September 2016. As they would both be able to use their respective annual exemptions of £3,000 for the 2016/17 tax year and for the 2015/16 tax year the value of the gift for IHT purposes would be zero.

Small Gifts: Legislation allows us to make gifts up to £250 to any one person in a tax year and such gifts would be free of IHT. If the value of the gift exceeds £250, then it cannot be used nor can it be used in conjunction with the annual exemption. It is therefore possible for you to make as many gifts of up to £250 to as many different people as you wish without IHT consequences.

Gifts out of normal expenditure of income: Now this is my favourite IHT exemption (I am sure that many lawyers will have their own as well). Basically, the law provides that if you make a gift and it is part of your normal settled expenditure, is made out of income and your standard of living is not affected then such gifts are free from IHT. This may be a useful allowance if say, you are retired and have a surplus of income over expenditure (so if you are retired and have a generous pension). It has been used by grandparents as an effective way to pay grandchildren's school fees.

It is important to note that your standard of living must not be affected. You cannot suddenly change from holidaying in the Maldives and dining out on steak and Rioja to not having holidays and existing on baked beans and water. Believe me some of my clients would do so if it could save their estates some IHT!

Gifts in consideration of marriage are exempt from IHT if the gifts are made:
- Before and conditional upon a particular marriage/civil partnership; or
- On or at the same time as the marriage/civil partnership; or
- After the marriage/civil partnership, but given in satisfaction if a prior obligation.

The gifts are limited to **£5,000** if made by a parent of one of the parties to the marriage/civil partnership, **£2,500** if made by a remoter ancestor of one of the parties (such as grandparents) and **£1,000** in all other cases.

So both sets of parents to the happy couple could give £10,000 to them without IHT implications (Lucky couple!).

Family maintenance: If a gift is made by one party in a marriage/civil partnership to the other party in favour of that party or a child of either party, and is for that person's maintenance, training or education then it will be IHT free. This is particularly useful if the parties were divorced as the spousal exemption referred to above would not apply. The exemption also applies to financial provision for dependant relatives so far as it is reasonable.

EXEMPTIONS AVAILABLE BOTH IN LIFETIME AND ON DEATH

Charity exemption: A gift to a charity is exempt from IHT as long as it is used exclusively for the benefit of the charity and is immediate. If you were to leave a minimum of 10 per cent of your estate to a charity or charities then your estate will benefit from a reduced rate of IHT at 36 per cent.

Spouse/civil partner exemption: Any gifts between spouses/civil partners are exempt from IHT. The gift must be immediate and can apply where the spouse is the beneficiary of/to benefit from a life interest trust created on death.

Agricultural Property Relief (APR): This is available for agricultural property such as land and pasture and certain buildings occupied in association with it (such as farmhouses, farm cottages and barns). Any cottages must be occupied for the purposes of agriculture.

The land needs to be occupied by the person making the gift/transfer for the period of **two** years immediately before the disposal or owned by that person for the **seven** years before the disposal and occupied by someone for agricultural purposes throughout that period.

APR is available at either 100 per cent or 50 per cent. If you think that APR would apply to your estate, I strongly suggest that you obtain professional guidance.

Business Property Relief (BPR): This is available at a rate of 100 per cent when the transferor has a business or interest in a business or shares in an unquoted company. It is available at a rate of 50 per cent in respect of shares in a quoted company (that gave that person control of the company) or on land, buildings and machinery used for a business undertaken by a company of which the transferor has control or a partnership if that person was a partner.

In order to be able to claim BPR the transferor must have owned the property for a period of two years immediately before the transfer. It is not available if the business undertaken consists wholly or mainly of either making or holding investments (such as a property holding company).

Again, if you are a business owner you need to seek advice from your lawyer and accountant on how best to structure your business interests.

RESIDENCE NIL RATE BAND

Tax does not have to be taxing....

According to Moria Stuart in the HMRC adverts. Someone should have reminded the Government about this when they concocted the Residence Nil Rate Band (RNRB).

ORIGIN

This can be traced back to the late summer of 2007, George Osborne declared that the Conservatives would raise the IHT threshold to £1 million and the general consensus is that this statement helped public favour turn slowly towards the Conservatives. This has now been delivered but in a somewhat convoluted way.

In the Summer Budget 2015, the Government introduced the RNRB as part of its 'commitment to reward work and support aspiration' and the RNRB 'takes the family home out of inheritance tax for all but the wealthiest'.

The Budget also confirmed the existing nil-rate band at £325,000 would remain frozen until the end of 2020/21.

WHAT IS THE RNRB?

HMRC's detailed proposal states the aim of the RNRB is 'to provide for an additional main residence nil-rate band for an estate if the deceased's interest in a residential property, which has been their residence at some point and is included in their estate, is left to one or more direct descendants on death.' This applies in respect of deaths on or after 6 April 2017.

The value of the RNRB will be 'the lower of the net value of the interest in the residential property (after deducting any liabilities such a mortgage) or the maximum amount of the band.' The maximum amount will be phased in as follows:
- £100,000 for 2017/18
- £125,000 for 2018/19
- £150,000 for 2019/20
- £175,000 for 2020/21

It will then increase in line with the CPI.

It will be limited to one residential property, if there is more than one residential property in the estate then the personal representatives can nominate which property qualifies. A buy-to-let property that the deceased never lived in will not qualify.

A direct descendent 'will be a child (including a step-child, adopted child or foster child) of the deceased and their lineal descendants.' This has been extended to spouses and civil partners of children (and their lineal descendants) and widows/widowers who have not remarried (in the case of pre-deceasing children).

Any unused proportion of RNRB can be transferred on the surviving spouse's death.

The relief will taper if 'the net value of the estate (after deducting any liabilities but before reliefs and exemptions) is above £2 million' by '£1 for every £2 that the net value exceeds that amount.'

There were concerns that the above may encourage individuals to remain in their properties to claim the RNRB rather than downsizing which may lead to a housing shortage. In September 2015, HMRC issued a technical note (confirmed in Clause 44 of the Finance Bill 2016). This provides that 'the qualifying conditions for the additional RNRB would be broadly the same as those for the RNRB', in that the:
- Individual dies on or after 6 April 2017.
- Property must have been owned by the individual and would have qualified for the RNRB had the individual retained it.
- Less valuable property, or other assets of an equivalent value if the property has been disposed of, are in the deceased's estate (including assets which are deemed to be part of a person's estate).
- Less valuable property, and any other assets of an equivalent value, are inherited by the individual's direct descendants on that person's death.

The following additional conditions would also apply:
- The downsizing or disposal occurs after 8 July 2015.
- Subject to the above, there would be no time limit on the period in which the downsizing or the disposals took place before death.
- There could be any number of downsizing moves between 8 July 2015 and the date of death.
- Downsizing would also include disposing of part of a property (including land occupied and used as a garden or grounds) or a share in it.
- Where a property is given away, assets of an equivalent value to the value of the property when the gift was made must be left to direct descendants.
- The value of the property would be the net value i.e. after deducting any mortgage or other debts charged on the property.
- The additional RNRB would be tapered away as the RNRB.
- The additional RNRB would be applied together with the available RNRB but the total for the two would still be capped so that they would not exceed the limit of the total available RNRB for a particular year.
- A claim would have to be made for the additional RNRB in a similar way that a claim is made to transfer any unused RNRB to the estate of a surviving spouse or civil partner.

Straightforward isn't it?

IS ALL THIS FAIR?

According to the Government, there is no evidence to 'suggest that the measure will have any significant adverse equalities impacts'.

However, I disagree, it is beneficial for married families with children but it does not help someone who has no direct descendants. What if a person has significant liquid assets but due to his/her job has never bought a property, the RNRB would not be available – is that fair? The same can be said for unmarried family members who want to leave their property to their nephews or nieces, again the RNRB would not be available.

"No will — no say"

4. Retain control beyond your mental capacity

People associate estate planning with events that happen after – not before – they die, such as the distribution of their estate. But loss of mental or physical capacity is a real risk that people face, and a risk that increases with age.

That's why you should make arrangements to cover a situation where you're still alive, but can no longer manage your own affairs. That's part of the planning process.

ACTION

Ask yourself these questions:

1. If I should lose the ability to manage my legal and financial affairs, who would act in my best interests?
2. If I were declared incapable of handling my estate, what would happen to my property if I made no arrangements?
3. What can I do to ensure my affairs are managed by someone competent, someone I trust?

POWERS OF ATTORNEY

In England and Wales, there are two types of Powers of Attorney. We have General Powers of Attorney and Lasting Powers of Attorney.

A *General* Power of Attorney is a cheap and cheerful way of legally authorising someone to make decisions on your behalf. Put simply they say that 'I X appoint you Y to be my lawful attorney'. They can be for a specific purpose, for example, signing documents on a house purchase if you are out of the country. So far so good, however, there is one major problem with a General Power of Attorney; it ceases to operate if you lose mental capacity.

In 2007, **Lasting** Powers of Attorney (LPAs) were introduced. The clue here is in the name; the authority conferred by the power of attorney lasts and continues to operate after you lose mental capacity.

LPAs replaced **Enduring** Powers of Attorney (EPAs). It is no longer possible to make an EPA, but existing EPAs made before I October 2007 remain valid. A valid EPA can be used by the attorney at any time, with the donor's knowledge and permission. However, if you begin to lose your mental capacity to manage your own affairs, your attorney becomes under a duty to register the EPA with the Office of the Public Guardian (OPG). The attorney cannot then use the power of attorney until the registration is complete. EPAs only relate to property and financial affairs.

LPAs are powerful legal documents. They allow you to choose people to act on your behalf should you later begin to lose your ability to manage your personal affairs because of physical or mental incapacity. They take effect, if need be, during your lifetime and are completely separate to a will.

Creating a LPA gives you the reassurance that you know who will make decisions for you once you cannot make them yourself. That person will be someone you know and trust to act in your best interests. Having the LPA in place saves considerable expense and time should your family later need to make decisions for you.

There are two types of LPA: one deals with your **property and financial affairs**, and the other with **health and welfare** issues.

An LPA can be created at any time while you have mental capacity, but can only be used once it has been registered at the OPG.

WHAT IS A PROPERTY AND FINANCIAL AFFAIRS LPA?

This type of LPA provides your attorney with authority to make decisions regarding your property and financial affairs. It can be created to suit your circumstances and can include, if you wish, restrictions on the powers you grant to your attorney.

Your attorneys will be able to make exactly the same decisions as you normally would, such as paying bills, making or selling investments, collecting benefits or selling your home.

A Property and Financial Affairs LPA is legally effective as soon as it is registered with the OPG, if you give your consent to your attorney acting for you.

While you have the necessary capacity, the LPA does not in any way prevent you from continuing to manage your own affairs should you wish. The LPA can only be used by your attorney without your permission once you lose the capacity to make your own decisions.

WHAT IS A HEALTH AND WELFARE LPA?

This type of LPA provides your attorney with authority to make decisions regarding personal issues, such as where you live or the type of care you receive. It can be expressly tailored to your personal circumstances. You can give your attorney the power to give or refuse consent for medical treatment, including an express statement about life sustaining treatment.

If you have already made a 'Living Will' (also known as an Advanced Treatment Directive or Advance Medical Decision) you should seek legal advice on how it will interact with, or be superseded by, a Health and Welfare LPA.

A Health and Welfare LPA must be registered with the OPG before it can be used. The registration may be done at any time. However, unlike a Property and Financial Affairs LPA, this type of LPA can only be used once you no longer have the capacity to manage your affairs yourself.

WHO CAN MAKE AN LPA?

Anyone aged 18 or over can make an LPA. You must make it as an individual – you cannot make a joint LPA. Anyone making an LPA must have mental capacity when making it.

LPAs cover people in England and Wales. An LPA made here may not be usable in any other country (including Scotland and Northern Ireland).

WHO CAN BE AN ATTORNEY?

You can choose any number of attorneys to act on your behalf, provided they are aged 18 or over. A Property and Financial Affairs LPA cannot appoint an attorney who is declared bankrupt at the time the form is signed. If you appoint more than one attorney, you will have to decide whether they must act together at all times, or whether they can act independently of each other.

You must take a great deal of time considering who should be your attorneys both for your property and financial affairs and for your health and welfare. This is because there is a great deal of interaction between the two roles.

You are perfectly within your rights to appoint different people to be your attorneys for your property and financial affairs and for your health and welfare, however problems could arise with this.

Example

Maurice has appointed his son Stephen to be his attorney for his property and financial affairs and his daughter Joanne to be his attorney for his health and welfare. The time comes when Maurice needs to go into care. Quite rightly Joanne starts looking for a suitable care home for her father. She finds a suitable care home for her father, but has to liaise with Stephen who holds the purse strings. He is of the opinion that the care home is too expensive and that Maurice's needs can be met by a cheaper care home. There is therefore an impasse while both attorneys try to reach an agreement which may not be in the best interests of Maurice.

You will see from the above example that it may be preferable to appoint the same attorneys for both your property and financial affairs and for your health and welfare decisions.

It is really important that your chosen attorneys agree to taking on this role and know what is involved. The attorneys should be people whom you trust completely to act in your best interests.

You can nominate substitute attorneys to act in the event that your first choice attorneys cannot act for any reasons.

WHAT MUST YOUR ATTORNEYS DO?

Before making decisions on your behalf, each attorney must understand and follow the principles, duties and regulations contained within the Mental Capacity Act 2005 and the associated code of practice. They must always act in your best interests and take due account of your needs.

Wherever possible, your attorneys must take all practical steps to help you make a particular decision. They must also take account of your past actions and present wishes.

Your attorneys must keep your money and your property separate from their own affairs and from those of other people. They must keep full and accurate accounts of all income and expenditure.

WHO ELSE IS INVOLVED?

Notified person
The LPA provides for you to nominate a person to be notified if the LPA is registered with the Office of the Public Guardian. This person has the right to object if they are concerned about the registration. After registration, they have no ongoing involvement in your affairs.

Certificate provider
A certificate provider is an independent third party who confirms that at the time you create the LPA:
- You understand the LPA and the powers it grants;
- You are not under any pressure to sign it; and
- You have the necessary mental capacity to create it.

The certificate provider can be your lawyer, your doctor, or someone who has known you for at least two years and who is not a relative. The certificate provider signs the LPA themselves before your attorneys sign.

REGISTERING THE LPA

Each LPA must be signed by you, your certificate provider, and your attorneys, in that order. You or your attorney can then send it to the Office of the Public Guardian for registration. The OPG's current fee for registration is (currently) £110 per LPA. The notified person must be informed at this time and has the opportunity to object to the registration.

Overall, the registration process can take around 10-12 weeks. It is therefore preferable to register the LPAs sooner rather than later, so that they can be used immediately if need be.

WHAT HAPPENS NEXT?

Once the LPA or preferably LPAs have been registered they can be used straight away or most likely they can be put in a safe place until needed. On the day that they are needed they will be worth their weight in gold.

Caution should be exercised in your choice of people, as these documents can be used to take financial advantage of the elderly. You might appoint one or more people – perhaps your partner, close friend, child/children or a trusted professional adviser, such as your lawyer. You can also appoint replacements if (for some reason) your first choice can't act.

Not only do you select **who** looks after your affairs, you can also direct the person you appoint on **how** you wish the power to be exercised.

AND IF YOU DON'T HAVE A LASTING POWER OF ATTORNEY

With no such document, your family (or health care provider) would have to apply to a tribunal or the courts to appoint a **deputy**. This costs money and can result in delaying the making of urgent decisions. Of course, you would have no say in who's appointed, or what they do with you or your assets. Once you've lost mental capacity through accident or the ageing process it's out of your control.

The lessons:
- Prepare these documents now while you can still make an informed decision without any undue pressure, and maximise the chances of making the right decision.
- Despite the risk of abuse they are invaluable.
- Minimise the risks by only appointing trusted people, preferably more than one jointly so they keep each other honest.

LIVING WILLS OR ADVANCED DECISIONS

In England and Wales, every mentally competent adult has a legal right to accept or refuse medical treatment, even if the refusal of that treatment leads to their death.

There are several terms used to describe the document by which you give directions about medical treatment. They're commonly called 'Living Wills' but are also referred to as 'Advanced Decisions'. They all have the same objectives:

- To protect **your right to refuse** unwanted medical treatment.
- To protect **your right to receive** desired medical treatment, and
- To ensure **you receive relief** from pain and suffering to the maximum extent that is reasonable in the circumstances.

Any medical professional providing treatment contrary to your health care directive is exposed to charges of assault, claims of negligence and/or breach of contract.

Usually these documents stipulate treatment *limitation* preferences, but they may indicate a wish that you want full measures taken to prolong your life, no matter what the treatment.

The medical treatment preferences can include for example:

- Preferences influenced by religious or other values and beliefs.
- Identifying living circumstances unacceptable to you arising from dependence on life-sustaining treatment, and
- Directing how far treatment should go when your condition is declared 'terminal', 'incurable' or 'irreversible'.

If you have appointed a health and welfare attorney, you need to make him/her aware of your wishes. If not s/he has (if you have authorised it in the LPA) a free hand in deciding what treatment you receive and s/he can refuse treatment for you (on your behalf).

"No will – no say"

5. Trusts

Before you begin reading this chapter, take a deep breath. It deals with one of the more complex aspects of estate planning. But having a basic understanding of the options offered is well worth the effort, even if you decide trusts aren't for you. An informed decision is better than an ill-informed decision to accept or reject.

The following as a whistle-stop tour of trusts and as with all the advice in this book, if you feel any of the options below may be appropriate for your circumstances, you should seek your own professional advice.

WHAT IS A TRUST?

A trust is a way of passing on assets without actually giving the ownership of the assets to your chosen beneficiaries.

You transfer the assets you wish to be given away (the 'trust fund') to the trustees, who hold it on behalf of the people who are to benefit from it — the beneficiaries — in accordance with the trust document.

A trust can be set up during your lifetime or in your will.

TRUSTEES' POWERS

Trustees can usually do anything with the trust fund, on behalf of the beneficiaries, that they could do with their own money. They may spend it, invest it, buy and insure property etc., as long as this is permitted by the terms of the trust. They may also distribute it to beneficiaries, but again only in accordance with the terms of the trust.

TRUSTEES' RESPONSIBILITIES

When they are appointed, each trustee has a duty to make sure that they understand the terms of the trust, and to review previous trustee activity to ensure that no breaches of trust have occurred in the past. Going forwards, trustees need to comply with the terms of the trust and all laws relating to trust administration – and in particular the statutory duty of care imposed by the Trustee Act 2000. This provides that a trustee must act with reasonable skill and care in carrying out their role, taking into account any special knowledge or experience they have.

The beneficiaries can take legal action against the trustees for any actions which are not authorised by the trust document or trust law. Trustees may have to personally reimburse any loss so incurred by the trust.

Unless the trust document provides otherwise, some general duties for trustees include:
- Not to make a personal profit from the trust, or have their personal interests conflict with those of the trust.
- To seek professional advice on matters in which they are not competent. This includes financial advice: Trustees have a duty to seek investment advice before using their power of investment and when periodically reviewing the investments, unless they formally conclude it is unnecessary to do so (e.g. if the fund is small and the cost of advice would outweigh the benefit to the fund). The advice must come from someone who is reasonably believed by the trustees to be qualified to give it, based on their ability in and practical experience of matters relating to the proposed investment. The Law Society views only independent financial advice to be proper advice.
- To consider the best interests of all the beneficiaries, not just one beneficiary or class of beneficiaries in particular.
- To keep records of trustee decisions and actions, and prepare trust accounts. Trustees are accountable to the beneficiaries.
- To insure trust property, investigate the condition of the property on an ongoing basis, and ensure that the title to the property and any other relevant documents are in order.
- To recover any debts due to the trust, and instigate legal proceedings if necessary. Trustees also have a duty to defend any action brought against them in their capacity as trustees. Trustees who participate in litigation should consider seeking protection against personal liability for adverse costs orders resulting from court proceedings.
- To declare any trust income or capital gains to HM Revenue and Customs, and pay any tax.

CAN TRUSTEES BE PAID?

Professional trustees can be paid, usually from trust funds, for services provided to or on behalf of a trust. Other trustees may not be paid for their time but can claim reasonable out of pocket expenses from the trust fund.

TRUSTEE LIABILITY

Trustees are personally liable for their actions and defaults as trustees. However, the trust document may contain a clause which seeks to limit or exclude this liability. In the absence of such a clause, trustees may wish to consider taking out insurance against any such liability.

TRUSTEE DELEGATION

Trustees cannot delegate the power to decide when and how the trust fund should be distributed.

They can delegate certain other functions, subject to the following safeguards:

- Delegation must not last more than 12 months.
- Notice of the delegation must be given to all co-trustees.
- The original trustee remains liable for the acts or defaults of the person taking on the delegated role.

Trustees may delegate their powers of investment and fund management to an agent, subject to a written Investment Policy Statement by which the agent must abide.

REPLACING A TRUSTEE

If a trustee is temporarily unable to act, certain powers may be delegated as explained above. If the trustee is regularly or permanently unable to act, retiring and being replaced would be preferable.

A trust can last for up to 125 years. While most end much sooner, there may come situations where a trustee needs to retire. Retiring trustees need to be protected from personal liability for any future breaches of trust; their replacement also needs to be protected from personal liability for breaches occurring before their appointment. Indemnities are put in place to ensure this.

LIFETIME TRUSTS

Two of the main reasons to create trusts in your lifetime would be to safeguard assets for beneficiaries and to potentially reduce your estate for inheritance tax. The main trusts that can be established are discretionary trusts and life interest trusts.

DISCRETIONARY TRUSTS

A discretionary trust is an extremely flexible form of trust, there is a pool of beneficiaries who all could benefit from the trust. No one beneficiary has a right to trust capital and they will only benefit if the trustees decide to release funds to them.

WHY SHOULD A DISCRETIONARY TRUST BE CREATED?

- Certain family members may not be able to manage money or may be encountering marital difficulties and the person creating the trust wants the flexibility afforded by the discretionary trust.
- For estate planning purposes.
- As discretionary trusts can last for up to 125 years they are a good way of protecting and managing family wealth.

INHERITANCE TAX IMPLICATIONS

If you create a discretionary trust during your lifetime, this is known as a Lifetime Chargeable Transfer (LCT). Insofar as the value of the transfers exceeds your available Nil Rate Band (see Chapter 3) inheritance tax (IHT) may be chargeable at a rate of 20 per cent. If you were to die within seven years of creating the trust it would be reassessed for IHT purposes.

During the lifetime of the trust, it will be assessed for IHT every 10 years (known as the periodic charge) and whenever capital leaves the trust (known as the exit charge). The calculations are quite complicated however (by way of illustration) the maximum rate for the periodic charge is 6 per cent.

If you decide to establish a discretionary trust, you have to weigh up the 'control' element against the IHT charge.

LIFE INTEREST TRUSTS

In essence a life interest trust provides an income (or a right to use a trust asset) for someone (say a spouse) for the rest of that person's life (the life tenant) whilst preserving the capital for other beneficiaries (remaindermen).

WHY SHOULD A LIFE INTEREST TRUST BE CREATED?

- To provide an income for a beneficiary without risking the capital.
- To provide a home for a beneficiary.
- For general estate planning.

INHERITANCE TAX IMPLICATIONS

Since the changes in the law contained in the Finance Act 2006, life interest trusts created in a lifetime are subject to IHT the same was as discretionary trusts.

WILL TRUSTS

There are various ways in which trusts can be used in your will to protect assets from the lifestyles of your chosen beneficiaries. I intend to cover the two main trusts that are used: Discretionary trusts and life interest trusts.

DISCRETIONARY TRUSTS

Discretionary trusts established in wills do not differ in substance to the ones created in life. The trust document will be the will and this will contain the trust details, such as the trustees and beneficiaries of the trust.

Again, the pool of beneficiaries only have a 'hope' of benefiting from the trust, it is up to the trustees to decide who is to receive any money from the trust. You are able to use a non-binding letter of wishes to let the trustees know what you would like them to do with the trust fund but this letter is not legally enforceable on them. This is why your choice of trustee is vitally important.

Discretionary trusts can often be used in wills where you have assets that would qualify for 100 per cent Business Property Relief (BPR) for inheritance tax (IHT). If you are married or in a civil partnership, rather than leaving these assets to your spouse (which would be spouse exempt for IHT), you can leave them to a discretionary trust and obtain BPR. This means that no IHT is payable and your spouse could still receive income from the assets. It also means that the assets could be ring fenced for future generations. The risk is that if you left the assets to your spouse and he/she died within two years the assets would not receive BPR on his/her death.

Discretionary trusts can be also used in complicated family situations where beneficiaries may not be able to handle money, may be encountering marital difficulties or may have personal issues such as alcohol or drug problems. A discretionary trust would allow the trustees to drip feed the inheritance to that beneficiary.

Furthermore, they can be very useful if you have young children and you want to ensure that they benefit from your estate but they are far too young for you to know if they will be mature enough to handle their inheritance. If, at the time of your death they are then the trust can simply be collapsed.

When a discretionary will trust is established on death the funds have come from the deceased's estate and IHT would have been paid as normal however moving on, the capital of the discretionary trust is not agreeable with the estate of any of the beneficiaries.

During the lifetime of the trust, there may be charges to IHT. There is an exit charge made every time trust property leaves the trust or when the trust comes to an end. There is also a periodic charge every ten years based on the value of the trust fund at that time. There will only ever be this charge if the value of the fund exceeds the nil rate band at that time. The calculations can be quite complicated however the maximum inheritance tax charge is 6 per cent, which people find reasonable given the amount of asset protection afforded by the discretionary trust structure.

LIFE INTEREST TRUSTS

These do not differ substantially to life interest trusts established in lifetime.

Life interest trust wills can be particularly useful in the case of people who have remarried and have children from their respective first relationships or in the case of a younger married couple where they are concerned that the surviving spouse may remarry and leave assets to the new spouse.

They provide a useful mechanism for protecting assets for the future generation whilst at the same time providing an income for the surviving spouse. These trusts can be drafted widely to provide a power to advance or loan capital to the life tenant or to advance capital to the remaindermen during the life tenant's lifetime (with their consent) such advancement can have potential IHT advantages (see the case study below).

For IHT tax purposes, on the death of the life tenant, he or she is treated as the owner of the trust capital and the value of the trust will be aggregated to their estate and any inheritance tax due would be apportioned pro rata between the trust and the estate. However, if the life interest trust was set up in favour of the spouse then on the first death there would have been no IHT due given the spousal exemption and on the life tenants death the transferable nil rate band should be available.

During the lifetime of the life tenant they can surrender or assign their life interest. This can offer estate planning opportunities as shown below.

CASE STUDY

THE SAVVY LIFE TENANT

Hilary married John later on in life. They had both been married before and had one child each from their previous relationships (Peter and Paul). They were independently wealthy and they went to see their lawyer to make wills.

Their priority was to ensure that the survivor of them was looked after and that Peter and Paul would inherit in due course. They were advised to execute life interest trust wills in favour of the survivor of them with the remaindermen being Peter and Paul.

John dies and the life interest trust comes into effect, the value of the trust fund when aggregated with Hilary's own assets is in excess of £800,000. Hilary is in good health and decides that she does not need recourse to all of the funds of the trust. She therefore decides to advance to Peter and Paul £100,000 each from the trust. She is deemed to have made a potentially exempt transfer and if she survives 7 years then the value of such gifts would fall outside of the inheritance net. Therefore the inheritance tax bill will be reduced from £60,000 to £0.

Life interest trusts also offer asset protection opportunities so if the life tenant were to remarry and then subsequently divorce as he/she does not own the underlying assets the capital assets can't be taken into account in divorce.

You could have a situation where the life tenant has his/her own wealth and does not need the income/capital from the trust.

OTHER TYPES OF TRUST

In wills, you are able to set up trusts for bereaved minors or bereaved young people. However, these are beyond the scope of this book. If you would like advice in respect of these, I suggest that you speak to a specialist lawyer.

"No will – no say"

7. Providing certainty for families who have a child with a disability

Parents, or anyone wishing to provide for a disabled child, grandchild or other relative with a disability, face a number of issues in planning for that child's future.

Let me set the scene for you. Parents of children with a disability find it hard to plan for their child's long term future: who'll care for their child when they can't, where will they live, will there be sufficient money for their care – how much is enough?

For many parents, their future is limited to getting through today.

Rarely do these parents have the time, or head space, to think about their own future. Issues such as financial planning for their own retirement or the basic preparation of a will and other essential succession planning needs don't see the light of day. Even the concept of retirement seems too remote to contemplate at all.

With no starting point to begin with, no end game they can identify and no milestones to measure progress along the way, it's simply been too hard. These families rank amongst those most in need of certainty and clarity around their family's future but have to live with a future clouded by uncertainty.

There are many issues that they face, in particular, receiving a large amount of money directly can affect the child's entitlement to means tested state benefits and Local Authority care.

Further, a disabled child may never be able to manage their own financial affairs. If money is left to them outright, then when they turn 18 someone may have to make a deputyship application to the Court of Protection to look after the money for them.

Trying to avoid these issues can still, without proper advice and planning, cause unforeseen problems later down the line.

Example: *if the parent leaves no money at all to the child, the Local Authority might bring a legal claim against the deceased parent's estate, as they have not provided for their child in their will.*

Parents also sometimes leave money to other people, in the hope that they will use it for the child. However, since the legacy will legally become that person's own money, they will be free to spend it how they wish and this may not be in the way the parent intended. Further, if that person later experiences matrimonial or financial difficulties, the money may become vulnerable in divorce or bankruptcy proceedings.

THE ANSWER: A TRUST

There is a solution which ensures that parents, or others wishing to provide for a disabled person, can have the peace of mind of knowing that they have provided for their child, while at the same time protecting any of the child's entitlement to state help. The child's share can be left to the child in trust. A trust is a means by which assets are held and managed by one or more people (the trustees) on behalf of someone else (the beneficiary).

HOW DOES A TRUST WORK?

The assets of the trust, while available to be used for the child's benefit, do not legally belong to the child. They are not assessed as the child's capital for means testing purposes under the current rules, and cannot be taken into account by the Department for Work and Pensions (DWP) or the Local Authority.

At the same time, although the legal title to the money rests with the trustees, the money does not actually belong to them and so would not be treated as theirs in the event of divorce or bankruptcy.

Parents, grandparents or anyone else wishing to provide for a disabled child should therefore always consider incorporating a trust in their wills.

WHAT CAN THE TRUSTEES DO WITH THE TRUST FUND?

The trustees can only use the money for the benefit of the trust beneficiaries, i.e. the disabled child or children. They might pay for clothes, equipment or holidays, make regular payments to the child's guardians, or contribute towards anything else the child needs.

The parent can name other family members, friends or even charities as potential trust beneficiaries, if they foresee them having a supporting role in caring for the child. This gives the trustees the discretion to use trust money for these other people too if they wish.

The parent may draft a non-binding, private, 'Letter of Wishes' to their trustees setting out how they would like the money to be used. Ultimately, though, the trustees decide how they should use the money in the best interests of the child.

WHO WILL BE INVOLVED?

The vital roles in the will are those of executors, trustees and guardians.

Executors are the people who administer your estate after your death. They will transfer the trust's share of your estate to your trustees.

Trustees are the people who deal with any trust established on your death. They are often the same people as your executors, but do not have to be. They must be people you completely trust, as they will have financial responsibility for the funds you leave in trust for your child. They can be family members, friends or professional trustees.

Guardians are legally responsible for the welfare and upbringing of young children. They will have parental responsibility until the child turns 18. If you die without appointing a guardian, the court will decide who will act, and this could be someone who is neither related nor known to your children. Your will can ensure that the guardians receive payments from funds left in trust for your children, to ensure they don't suffer financial hardship from taking on the guardian role. These payments can be regular, covering clothing, food, transportation and other maintenance payments, or one-off payments covering specialist medical equipment or house adaptations. The trustees have the final say on the amount and frequency of any payments.

Your guardians can be the same people as your executors and/or trustees, but it is important that there are checks and balances in place on any payments made out of your children's money. I would generally advise that separate people are appointed as trustees and guardians.

Both guardians and trustees will have ongoing roles throughout your child's life, so choosing people you know and trust to act in your child's best interests is crucial.

WHAT ELSE SHOULD BE CONSIDERED?

Life insurance – aside from assets left under your will, consider taking out a life insurance policy which would pay out in the event of your death. The policy could provide funds to meet the ongoing expenses associated with bringing up a child, particularly one with physical or mental disabilities. You may be surprised but the cost of the policy (depending on your circumstances) may not be high. As with everything in this book you should seek advice from a suitably qualified and regulated adviser.

Financial Advice – it goes without saying that families should speak with an independent financial adviser to help build a comprehensive financial and succession plan that provides for the parents future and the integrated support for their child's long term care even after they pass away.

Once such a plan is created specialist estate planning legal advice and documentation to underpin the families' plans needs to be taken. All the potential legal ramifications are considered while wills, Lasting Powers of Attorney and other family agreements are individually tailored to include all elements of the agreed plan.

SUMMARY

I've walked you through a legal minefield, pointing out some areas that need special consideration.

You could certainly attempt to take care of some of this yourself, but as you have read, certain finesse is required in dealing with more complicated areas. Even homemade wills are fraught with danger. Remember, you don't know what you don't know!

FINAL RULE The more complex your personal or financial affairs, the more likely you'll require professional advice. Only then can you be certain that your will is to be done properly and your broader estate planning needs satisfied.

SCHEDULE I

A check list of succession planning issues for consideration and (as appropriate) discussion with family members, or your professional advisers:

1. **Protecting family wealth from:**
   - A beneficiary's marriage failing.
   - A beneficiary becoming bankrupt.
   - A beneficiary being sued.
   - A beneficiary's mental incapacity.
   - A beneficiary being a spendthrift.
   - A beneficiary being drug or gambling dependent.
   - The risk associated with a spouse remarrying.
   - A beneficiary being vulnerable for some other reason.
   - Intestacy of beneficiaries.

2. **Minimising family disputes**
   - Treat beneficiaries fairly/equally and, if not, how to minimise risk of successful challenge.
   - Document your rationale for decisions.
   - Communicate intentions to beneficiaries – avoid surprises, unless of course they're nice surprises.
   - Clarify treatment of gifts made during their lifetime – are they to be treated as an advance on an inheritance or in addition to an inheritance.
   - Provide more to younger beneficiaries so they don't have to pay for their education out of their inheritance (when older siblings had that advantage while you were alive).
   - Fair distribution of family heirlooms.
   - Make special provision for family business.
   - Make special provision for large assets.
   - Address loans given to beneficiaries.
   - Allow for capital gains tax.
   - Avoid conflicts of interest for executors and attorney.

3. **Cater for the needs of a blended family**
   - Provide for children from a prior marriage.
   - Balance needs of partner with children and step-children.
   - Keeping family assets within your bloodline.
   - Communicate plans to extended family to avoid disputes.
   - Use of mutual wills or life interest trust wills to preserve assets for children when a spouse passes, especially in blended family situations.

4. **Ensure dependants are cared for**
   - Nominate appropriate guardians.
   - Communicate wishes to guardians.
   - Boost estate funding to meet needs of beneficiaries using life insurance.

5. **Reduce the chance of successful claims against estate**
   - Anticipate and address likely claims.
   - Execute the will properly.
   - Store the will safely (you can't imagine how many wills are lost).
   - Document justification, that is write out or otherwise document the reasons for your actions.
   - Communicate with beneficiaries while you're alive about your will.
   - Get advice on likely claims.

6. **Protect vulnerable beneficiaries**
   - Financial protection for the disabled.
   - Appoint appropriate guardians for minors.
   - Create disability trust during your lifetime or in your will.
   - Ongoing care for disabled adult beneficiaries.
   - Boost size of estate to provide for beneficiaries using life insurance.

7. **Optimise financial outcomes for beneficiaries**
   - Co-ordinate specialist tax, legal, investment and planning advice for executor.
   - Administer estate in tax effective manner.
   - Integrate estate administration with appropriate strategies for beneficiaries.

8. **Assist children and grandchildren with education and housing**
   - Whilst you're alive.
   - In the event of your death.
   - In the event of your children predeceasing you.

9. **Support philanthropy**
   - Support philanthropy tax effectively during your life.
   - Support philanthropy via your estate.
   - Create a lasting legacy through charitable giving (e.g. a gift to the Red Cross).

10. **Optimise benefit from future inheritance**
    - Protect inheritance from claims against the deceased's estate.
    - Protect inheritance from creditors.
    - Protect inheritance from legal action.
    - Minimise taxation on inheritance.

II. Protect family business interests
- Plan for business succession.
- Ensure business succession integrates with your estate planning.
- Protect against key-person risk.

12. Implement appropriate powers of attorney
- For property and financial matters.
- For health and welfare matters.

| "No will — no say"

SCHEDULE 2

The three stage process of succession planning:

1. **Identification of personal assets** and those in your broader estate such as assets owned jointly, or owned by trusts or companies.

2. **Identification of potential risks** including, for example, your early death or the possible divorce or bankruptcy of a beneficiary.

3. **Design and implementation of a plan** that incorporates all of your assets and takes into account flexibility to accommodate future changes, risk minimisation, tax minimisation and succession issues.

Each step is a multi-disciplinary exercise that usually will require the co-ordinated involvement of your lawyer, independent financial adviser and accountant.

SCHEDULE 3

ESTATE PLANNING SELF ASSESSMENT

Please complete details that are applicable to you. A 'Yes' answer to any question indicates you require specialist advice before you complete a will.

	PLEASE ANSWER THE FOLLOWING QUESTIONS	YES/NO
	If you have a spouse or co-habit with your partner	
1	Does your partner have a condition that affects, or with the passing of time could affect, his/her **mental capacity** (e.g., Alzheimer's disease)?	
2	Does your partner have serious **problems handling money**, to the point where you would not want him/her having direct access to the assets in your estate?	
3	Are you and your partner having serious **relationship problems**, to the point where you are concerned that you and he/she might separate?	
4	Are there any other reasons why you might want to **exclude your partner** from your will or limit the gift you make to him/her from your estate?	
5	Are you responsible for the **care** and upbringing of **someone else's child** (i.e., a child who is not your natural or adopted child)?	
6	Have you had a **son or daughter die leaving behind a child** or children of his or her own (i.e., do you have a grandchild or grandchildren from a son or daughter who has since died)?	
	If you have a blended family	
7	Does your partner have any **children from another relationship** (i.e., children that are not your natural or adopted children)?	
8	Do you have any **children from another relationship** (i.e., children that are not your current spouse/partner's natural or adopted children)?	

	If children may benefit	
9	Do you have a **child with a disorder** for whom special arrangements are needed in your will?	
10	Do you have a child who has **serious problems handling money** and who you would not want having direct access to the assets in your estate?	
11	Do you have a child who is married or in a committed domestic relationship and having serious **relationship problems** with his/her spouse/partner, to the point where you are concerned that they might separate?	
12	Do you have a child whom you want to **exclude from your will** or give a much smaller share of your estate than your other children?	
	Other Issues	
13	Do you wish to make a **specific gift** to someone when you die, even if your spouse/partner survives you?	
14	Do you want to leave someone a **gift** in your will that is **subject to** them satisfying a particular condition (other than them living longer than you and/or reaching a given age)?	
15	Do you want to leave someone a **'life interest'** (i.e., a gift of assets or a share of your estate which they enjoy while they are alive and which passes automatically to someone else when they die)?	
16	Do you want to leave a **gift of specific shares** in a company or other securities to someone in your will?	
17	Do you want to leave a **gift of specific real estate** to someone in your will?	
18	Do you want to make a **gift** to a beneficiary **subject to them taking over a debt** or mortgage (rather than that debt or mortgage being paid out by your estate, which is what would normally happen)?	
19	Do you or your spouse/partner control a **family company** or have shares in any private (non-listed) company that may need special consideration in your will?	
20	Do you or your spouse/partner control a **family trust** or have units in any private (non-listed) unit trust that may need special consideration in your will?	

21	Do you or your spouse/partner operate a business or have an interest as a partner in a **partnership** that may need special consideration in your will?	
22	Do you or your spouse/partner own **substantial assets**, especially real estate, **outside England and Wales**?	
23	Are you or your spouse/partner subject to any **agreement or court order** that restricts your ability to transfer your assets or that could otherwise affect the distribution of your estate	
24	**Discretionary trusts (see notes below)** Do you want to include a discretionary trust in your will? *	

* If
- your estate is substantial; and/or
- income producing assets will be left to beneficiaries; and/or
- one or more beneficiary is at risk of divorce, bankruptcy, is a spendthrift,
  suffers a mental incapacity, or has a gambling, drug or alcohol dependency,
- one or more beneficiary is under the influence of a person you are concerned about,

then you should consider including a discretionary trust in your will. In many circumstances substantial tax benefits and asset protection can be achieved by distributing assets to a trust rather than individual beneficiaries. The benefits, structure and type of trust vary with the circumstances.